TABLES CHAMPION

TABLES FOR THIRD CLASS

Editor: Donna Garvin
Design: Philip Ryan Graphic Design
Layout: The Unlimited Design Co.
Illustrations: Emily Skinner (GCI)
Cover illustration: Martin Remphry (GCI)

ISBN: 978-1-908507-25-9

Printed in Ireland by Walsh Colour Print, Castleisland, County Kerry. Freephone 1800 613 111.

educate.ie

Week by week at a glance:

Addition Tables	
Subtraction Tables	
Multiplication Tables	
Division Tables	
Week 1	Revision 2+, –2
Week 2	Revision 3+, –3
Week 3	Revision 4+, –4
Week 4	Revision 5+, –5
Week 5	Revision 6+, –6
Week 6	Revision 7+, –7
Week 7	Revision 8+, –8
Week 8	Revision 9+, –9
Week 9	Revision 10+, –10
Week 10	Look Back
Check-up 1	
Week 11	Multiplication ×2
Week 12	Multiplication ×4
Week 13	Multiplication ×8
Week 14	Multiplication ×5
Week 15	Multiplication ×10
Check-up 2	
Week 16	Multiplication ×3
Week 17	Multiplication ×6
Week 18	Multiplication ×9
Week 19	Multiplication ×7
Week 20	Look Back
Check-up 3	
Week 21	Multiplication and Division ×2, ÷2
Week 22	Multiplication and Division ×3, ÷3
Week 23	Multiplication and Division ×4, ÷4
Week 24	Multiplication and Division ×5, ÷5
Week 25	Multiplication and Division ×6, ÷6
Week 26	Multiplication and Division ×7, ÷7
Week 27	Multiplication and Division ×8, ÷8
Week 28	Multiplication and Division ×9, ÷9
Week 29	Multiplication and Division ×10, ÷10
Week 30	Look Back
Check-up 4	

Note for Teachers:
You may choose to cover the week-by-week scheme in a different order, according to your teaching plan. Also, if you wish, the answers can be downloaded from the educate.ie website. As for the time allowed for each daily test, Teachers might find it beneficial on occasions to allow the pupils to set their own target time.

Tables

Addition 1 to 10

1 +	2 +	3 +	4 +	5 +
1 + 0 = 1	2 + 0 = 2	3 + 0 = 3	4 + 0 = 4	5 + 0 = 5
1 + 1 = 2	2 + 1 = 3	3 + 1 = 4	4 + 1 = 5	5 + 1 = 6
1 + 2 = 3	2 + 2 = 4	3 + 2 = 5	4 + 2 = 6	5 + 2 = 7
1 + 3 = 4	2 + 3 = 5	3 + 3 = 6	4 + 3 = 7	5 + 3 = 8
1 + 4 = 5	2 + 4 = 6	3 + 4 = 7	4 + 4 = 8	5 + 4 = 9
1 + 5 = 6	2 + 5 = 7	3 + 5 = 8	4 + 5 = 9	5 + 5 = 10
1 + 6 = 7	2 + 6 = 8	3 + 6 = 9	4 + 6 = 10	5 + 6 = 11
1 + 7 = 8	2 + 7 = 9	3 + 7 = 10	4 + 7 = 11	5 + 7 = 12
1 + 8 = 9	2 + 8 = 10	3 + 8 = 11	4 + 8 = 12	5 + 8 = 13
1 + 9 = 10	2 + 9 = 11	3 + 9 = 12	4 + 9 = 13	5 + 9 = 14
1 + 10 = 11	2 + 10 = 12	3 + 10 = 13	4 + 10 = 14	5 + 10 = 15

6 +	7 +	8 +	9 +	10 +
6 + 0 = 6	7 + 0 = 7	8 + 0 = 8	9 + 0 = 9	10 + 0 = 10
6 + 1 = 7	7 + 1 = 8	8 + 1 = 9	9 + 1 = 10	10 + 1 = 11
6 + 2 = 8	7 + 2 = 9	8 + 2 = 10	9 + 2 = 11	10 + 2 = 12
6 + 3 = 9	7 + 3 = 10	8 + 3 = 11	9 + 3 = 12	10 + 3 = 13
6 + 4 = 10	7 + 4 = 11	8 + 4 = 12	9 + 4 = 13	10 + 4 = 14
6 + 5 = 11	7 + 5 = 12	8 + 5 = 13	9 + 5 = 14	10 + 5 = 15
6 + 6 = 12	7 + 6 = 13	8 + 6 = 14	9 + 6 = 15	10 + 6 = 16
6 + 7 = 13	7 + 7 = 14	8 + 7 = 15	9 + 7 = 16	10 + 7 = 17
6 + 8 = 14	7 + 8 = 15	8 + 8 = 16	9 + 8 = 17	10 + 8 = 18
6 + 9 = 15	7 + 9 = 16	8 + 9 = 17	9 + 9 = 18	10 + 9 = 19
6 + 10 = 16	7 + 10 = 17	8 + 10 = 18	9 + 10 = 19	10 + 10 = 20

Tables

Subtraction 1 to 10

− 1	− 2	− 3	− 4	− 5
1 − 1 = 0	2 − 2 = 0	3 − 3 = 0	4 − 4 = 0	5 − 5 = 0
2 − 1 = 1	3 − 2 = 1	4 − 3 = 1	5 − 4 = 1	6 − 5 = 1
3 − 1 = 2	4 − 2 = 2	5 − 3 = 2	6 − 4 = 2	7 − 5 = 2
4 − 1 = 3	5 − 2 = 3	6 − 3 = 3	7 − 4 = 3	8 − 5 = 3
5 − 1 = 4	6 − 2 = 4	7 − 3 = 4	8 − 4 = 4	9 − 5 = 4
6 − 1 = 5	7 − 2 = 5	8 − 3 = 5	9 − 4 = 5	10 − 5 = 5
7 − 1 = 6	8 − 2 = 6	9 − 3 = 6	10 − 4 = 6	11 − 5 = 6
8 − 1 = 7	9 − 2 = 7	10 − 3 = 7	11 − 4 = 7	12 − 5 = 7
9 − 1 = 8	10 − 2 = 8	11 − 3 = 8	12 − 4 = 8	13 − 5 = 8
10 − 1 = 9	11 − 2 = 9	12 − 3 = 9	13 − 4 = 9	14 − 5 = 9
11 − 1 = 10	12 − 2 = 10	13 − 3 = 10	14 − 4 = 10	15 − 5 = 10

− 6	− 7	− 8	− 9	− 10
6 − 6 = 0	7 − 7 = 0	8 − 8 = 0	9 − 9 = 0	10 − 10 = 0
7 − 6 = 1	8 − 7 = 1	9 − 8 = 1	10 − 9 = 1	11 − 10 = 1
8 − 6 = 2	9 − 7 = 2	10 − 8 = 2	11 − 9 = 2	12 − 10 = 2
9 − 6 = 3	10 − 7 = 3	11 − 8 = 3	12 − 9 = 3	13 − 10 = 3
10 − 6 = 4	11 − 7 = 4	12 − 8 = 4	13 − 9 = 4	14 − 10 = 4
11 − 6 = 5	12 − 7 = 5	13 − 8 = 5	14 − 9 = 5	15 − 10 = 5
12 − 6 = 6	13 − 7 = 6	14 − 8 = 6	15 − 9 = 6	16 − 10 = 6
13 − 6 = 7	14 − 7 = 7	15 − 8 = 7	16 − 9 = 7	17 − 10 = 7
14 − 6 = 8	15 − 7 = 8	16 − 8 = 8	17 − 9 = 8	18 − 10 = 8
15 − 6 = 9	16 − 7 = 9	17 − 8 = 9	18 − 9 = 9	19 − 10 = 9
16 − 6 = 10	17 − 7 = 10	18 − 8 = 10	19 − 9 = 10	20 − 10 = 10

Tables

Multiplication 2 to 10

× 2	× 3	× 4	× 5	× 6
0 × 2 = 0	0 × 3 = 0	0 × 4 = 0	0 × 5 = 0	0 × 6 = 0
1 × 2 = 2	1 × 3 = 3	1 × 4 = 4	1 × 5 = 5	1 × 6 = 6
2 × 2 = 4	2 × 3 = 6	2 × 4 = 8	2 × 5 = 10	2 × 6 = 12
3 × 2 = 6	3 × 3 = 9	3 × 4 = 12	3 × 5 = 15	3 × 6 = 18
4 × 2 = 8	4 × 3 = 12	4 × 4 = 16	4 × 5 = 20	4 × 6 = 24
5 × 2 = 10	5 × 3 = 15	5 × 4 = 20	5 × 5 = 25	5 × 6 = 30
6 × 2 = 12	6 × 3 = 18	6 × 4 = 24	6 × 5 = 30	6 × 6 = 36
7 × 2 = 14	7 × 3 = 21	7 × 4 = 28	7 × 5 = 35	7 × 6 = 42
8 × 2 = 16	8 × 3 = 24	8 × 4 = 32	8 × 5 = 40	8 × 6 = 48
9 × 2 = 18	9 × 3 = 27	9 × 4 = 36	9 × 5 = 45	9 × 6 = 54
10 × 2 = 20	10 × 3 = 30	10 × 4 = 40	10 × 5 = 50	10 × 6 = 60

× 7	× 8	× 9	× 10
0 × 7 = 0	0 × 8 = 0	0 × 9 = 0	0 × 10 = 0
1 × 7 = 7	1 × 8 = 8	1 × 9 = 9	1 × 10 = 10
2 × 7 = 14	2 × 8 = 16	2 × 9 = 18	2 × 10 = 20
3 × 7 = 21	3 × 8 = 24	3 × 9 = 27	3 × 10 = 30
4 × 7 = 28	4 × 8 = 32	4 × 9 = 36	4 × 10 = 40
5 × 7 = 35	5 × 8 = 40	5 × 9 = 45	5 × 10 = 50
6 × 7 = 42	6 × 8 = 48	6 × 9 = 54	6 × 10 = 60
7 × 7 = 49	7 × 8 = 56	7 × 9 = 63	7 × 10 = 70
8 × 7 = 56	8 × 8 = 64	8 × 9 = 72	8 × 10 = 80
9 × 7 = 63	9 × 8 = 72	9 × 9 = 81	9 × 10 = 90
10 × 7 = 70	10 × 8 = 80	10 × 9 = 90	10 × 10 = 100

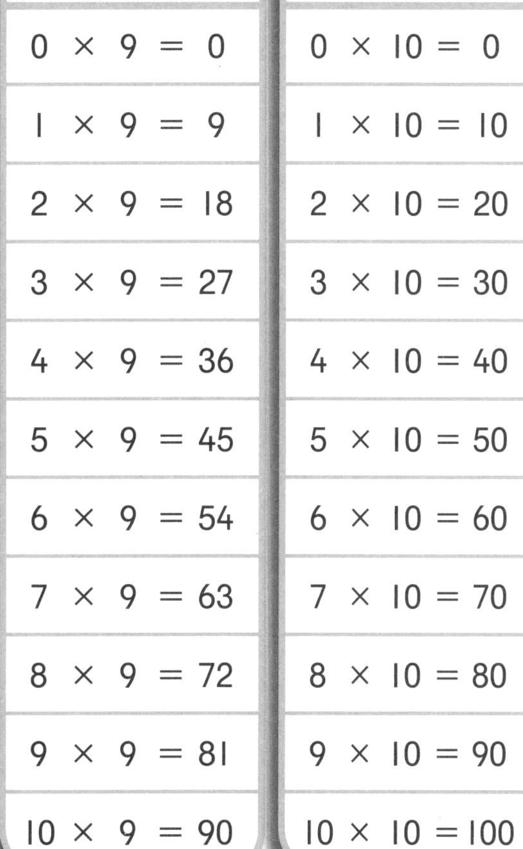

Tables — Division 2 to 10

÷ 2	÷ 3	÷ 4	÷ 5	÷ 6
2 ÷ 2 = 1	3 ÷ 3 = 1	4 ÷ 4 = 1	5 ÷ 5 = 1	6 ÷ 6 = 1
4 ÷ 2 = 2	6 ÷ 3 = 2	8 ÷ 4 = 2	10 ÷ 5 = 2	12 ÷ 6 = 2
6 ÷ 2 = 3	9 ÷ 3 = 3	12 ÷ 4 = 3	15 ÷ 5 = 3	18 ÷ 6 = 3
8 ÷ 2 = 4	12 ÷ 3 = 4	16 ÷ 4 = 4	20 ÷ 5 = 4	24 ÷ 6 = 4
10 ÷ 2 = 5	15 ÷ 3 = 5	20 ÷ 4 = 5	25 ÷ 5 = 5	30 ÷ 6 = 5
12 ÷ 2 = 6	18 ÷ 3 = 6	24 ÷ 4 = 6	30 ÷ 5 = 6	36 ÷ 6 = 6
14 ÷ 2 = 7	21 ÷ 3 = 7	28 ÷ 4 = 7	35 ÷ 5 = 7	42 ÷ 6 = 7
16 ÷ 2 = 8	24 ÷ 3 = 8	32 ÷ 4 = 8	40 ÷ 5 = 8	48 ÷ 6 = 8
18 ÷ 2 = 9	27 ÷ 3 = 9	36 ÷ 4 = 9	45 ÷ 5 = 9	54 ÷ 6 = 9
20 ÷ 2 = 10	30 ÷ 3 = 10	40 ÷ 4 = 10	50 ÷ 5 = 10	60 ÷ 6 = 10

÷ 7	÷ 8	÷ 9	÷ 10
7 ÷ 7 = 1	8 ÷ 8 = 1	9 ÷ 9 = 1	10 ÷ 10 = 1
14 ÷ 7 = 2	16 ÷ 8 = 2	18 ÷ 9 = 2	20 ÷ 10 = 2
21 ÷ 7 = 3	24 ÷ 8 = 3	27 ÷ 9 = 3	30 ÷ 10 = 3
28 ÷ 7 = 4	32 ÷ 8 = 4	36 ÷ 9 = 4	40 ÷ 10 = 4
35 ÷ 7 = 5	40 ÷ 8 = 5	45 ÷ 9 = 5	50 ÷ 10 = 5
42 ÷ 7 = 6	48 ÷ 8 = 6	54 ÷ 9 = 6	60 ÷ 10 = 6
49 ÷ 7 = 7	56 ÷ 8 = 7	63 ÷ 9 = 7	70 ÷ 10 = 7
56 ÷ 7 = 8	64 ÷ 8 = 8	72 ÷ 9 = 8	80 ÷ 10 = 8
63 ÷ 7 = 9	72 ÷ 8 = 9	81 ÷ 9 = 9	90 ÷ 10 = 9
70 ÷ 7 = 10	80 ÷ 8 = 10	90 ÷ 9 = 10	100 ÷ 10 = 10

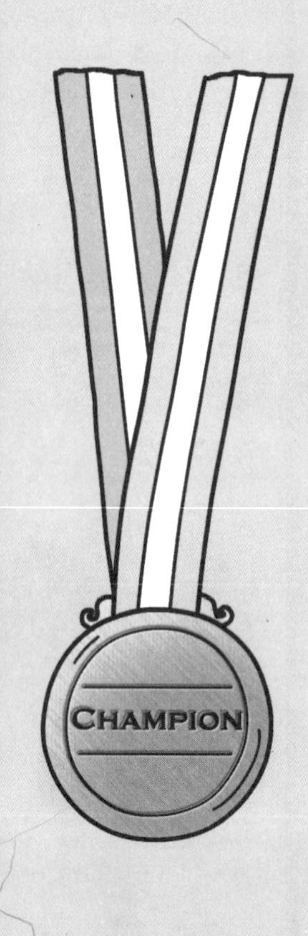

Week 1

2+, −2 Revision

Weekly Assessment

Monday

Time allowed: minutes

1.	2 + 5 = ___
2.	2 + 7 = ___
3.	2 + 2 = ___
4.	2 + 10 = ___
5.	2 + 6 = ___
6.	2 + 8 = ___
7.	2 + 3 = ___
8.	2 + 4 = ___
9.	2 + 0 = ___
10.	2 + 9 = ___
11.	1 + 2 = ___
12.	6 + 2 = ___
13.	8 + 2 = ___
14.	0 + 2 = ___
15.	10 + 2 = ___
16.	3 + 2 = ___
17.	7 + 2 = ___
18.	4 + 2 = ___
19.	9 + 2 = ___
20.	5 + 2 = ___

Score ___ / 20

Tuesday

Time allowed: minutes

1.	2 + ___ = 6
2.	2 + ___ = 2
3.	2 + ___ = 9
4.	2 + ___ = 11
5.	2 + ___ = 5
6.	2 + ___ = 8
7.	2 + ___ = 12
8.	2 + ___ = 4
9.	2 + ___ = 7
10.	2 + ___ = 10
11.	___ + 2 = 9
12.	___ + 2 = 5
13.	___ + 2 = 7
14.	___ + 2 = 11
15.	___ + 2 = 3
16.	___ + 2 = 8
17.	___ + 2 = 12
18.	___ + 2 = 6
19.	___ + 2 = 4
20.	___ + 2 = 10

Score ___ / 20

Wednesday

Time allowed: minutes

1.	9 − 2 = ___
2.	4 − 2 = ___
3.	11 − 2 = ___
4.	7 − 2 = ___
5.	2 − 2 = ___
6.	12 − 2 = ___
7.	5 − 2 = ___
8.	8 − 2 = ___
9.	10 − 2 = ___
10.	6 − 2 = ___
11.	___ − 2 = 8
12.	___ − 2 = 10
13.	___ − 2 = 4
14.	___ − 2 = 7
15.	___ − 2 = 9
16.	___ − 2 = 5
17.	___ − 2 = 1
18.	___ − 2 = 3
19.	___ − 2 = 6
20.	___ − 2 = 0

Score ___ / 20

Thursday

Time allowed: minutes

1.	2 + 7 = ___
2.	2 + 0 = ___
3.	2 + 3 = ___
4.	2 + 8 = ___
5.	2 + 6 = ___
6.	2 + 9 = ___
7.	2 + 2 = ___
8.	2 + 4 = ___
9.	2 + 10 = ___
10.	2 + 5 = ___
11.	___ + 2 = 8
12.	___ + 2 = 11
13.	___ + 2 = 10
14.	2 + ___ = 5
15.	2 + ___ = 9
16.	___ − 2 = 8
17.	___ − 2 = 6
18.	___ − 2 = 10
19.	___ − ___ = 4
20.	___ − ___ = 0

Score ___ / 20

Week 2

3+, –3 Revision

Weekly Assessment ☹ ☐ 😐 ☐ ☺ ☐

	Monday		Tuesday		Wednesday		Thursday
	Time allowed: 1:35 minutes		Time allowed: 1:3 minutes		Time allowed: minutes		Time allowed: 3:30 minutes
1.	3 + 10 = 13	1.	3 + 5 = 8	1.	10 – 3 = 7	1.	3 + 6 = 9
2.	3 + 4 = 7	2.	3 + 7 = 10	2.	6 – 3 = 3	2.	3 + 3 = 6
3.	3 + 6 = 9	3.	3 + 0 = 3	3.	11 – 3 =	3.	3 + 5 = 8
4.	3 + 0 = 3	4.	3 + 16 = 13	4.	7 – 3 =	4.	3 + 9 = 12
5.	3 + 7 = 10	5.	3 + 4 = 7	5.	12 – 3 =	5.	3 + 7 = 10
6.	3 + 3 = 6	6.	3 + 6 = 9	6.	3 – 3 =	6.	3 + 10 = 13
7.	3 + 5 = 8	7.	3 + 9 = 12	7.	8 – 3 =	7.	3 + 0 = 3
8.	3 + 9 = 12	8.	3 + 2 = 5	8.	13 – 3 =	8.	3 + 4 = 7
9.	3 + 2 = 5	9.	3 + 8 = 11	9.	5 – 3 =	9.	3 + 2 = 5
10.	3 + 8 = 11	10.	3 + 3 = 6	10.	9 – 3 =	10.	3 + 8 = 11
11.	6 + 3 = 9	11.	9 + 3 = 12	11.	– 3 = 2	11.	1 + 3 = 4
12.	7 + 3 = 10	12.	1 + 3 = 4	12.	– 3 = 5	12.	7 + 3 = 10
13.	1 + 3 = 4	13.	8 + 3 = 11	13.	– 3 = 10	13.	0 + 3 = 3
14.	9 + 3 = 12	14.	4 + 3 = 7	14.	– 3 = 1	14.	3 + 5 = 8
15.	5 + 3 = 8	15.	10 + 3 = 13	15.	– 3 = 6	15.	3 + 6 = 9
16.	10 + 3 = 13	16.	2 + 3 = 5	16.	– 3 = 9	16.	8 – 3 = 5
17.	3 + 3 = 6	17.	7 + 3 = 10	17.	– 3 = 4	17.	7 – 3 = 4
18.	4 + 3 = 7	18.	5 + 3 = 8	18.	– 3 = 7	18.	10 – 3 = 7
19.	0 + 3 = 3	19.	3 + 3 = 6	19.	– 3 = 3	19.	12 – 3 = 9
20.	8 + 3 = 11	20.	6 + 3 = 9	20.	– 3 = 8	20.	8 – 3 = 6
	Score 20/20		Score 20/20		Score ___/20		Score ___/20

Week 3

4+, −4 Revision

Weekly Assessment

	Monday	Tuesday	Wednesday	Thursday
	Time allowed: minutes	Time allowed: minutes	Time allowed: minutes	Time allowed: minutes
1.	4 + 5 =	4 + = 12	12 − 4 =	4 + 6 =
2.	4 + 1 =	4 + = 6	4 − 4 =	4 + 2 =
3.	4 + 8 =	4 + = 11	11 − 4 =	4 + 5 =
4.	4 + 4 =	4 + = 7	8 − 4 =	4 + 8 =
5.	4 + 9 =	4 + = 13	13 − 4 =	4 + 4 =
6.	4 + 2 =	4 + = 4	9 − 4 =	4 + 7 =
7.	4 + 10 =	4 + = 9	7 − 4 =	4 + 10 =
8.	4 + 6 =	4 + = 14	10 − 4 =	4 + 3 =
9.	4 + 3 =	4 + = 10	6 − 4 =	4 + 0 =
10.	4 + 7 =	4 + = 8	14 − 4 =	4 + 9 =
11.	6 + 4 =	+ 4 = 12	− 4 = 10	+ 4 = 8
12.	4 + 4 =	+ 4 = 7	− 4 = 2	+ 4 = 5
13.	8 + 4 =	+ 4 = 13	− 4 = 6	+ 4 = 12
14.	0 + 4 =	+ 4 = 9	− 4 = 0	4 + = 7
15.	5 + 4 =	+ 4 = 14	− 4 = 7	4 + = 10
16.	2 + 4 =	+ 4 = 5	− 4 = 4	− 4 = 9
17.	9 + 4 =	+ 4 = 10	− 4 = 9	− 4 = 0
18.	7 + 4 =	+ 4 = 8	− 4 = 3	− 4 = 10
19.	10 + 4 =	+ 4 = 6	− 4 = 5	− 4 = 6
20.	3 + 4 =	+ 4 = 11	− 4 = 8	− 4 = 3
	Score ___ / 20	Score ___ / 20	Score ___ / 20	Score ___ / 20

Week 4

5+, −5 Revision

Weekly Assessment ☹ ☐ 😐 ☐ ☺ ☐

	Monday	Tuesday	Wednesday	Thursday
	Time allowed: ___ minutes	Time allowed: ___ minutes	Time allowed: ___ minutes	Time allowed: ___ minutes
1.	5 + 5 = ___	5 + ___ = 11	15 − 5 = ___	5 + 7 = ___
2.	5 + 0 = ___	5 + ___ = 7	9 − 5 = ___	5 + 2 = ___
3.	5 + 4 = ___	5 + ___ = 13	10 − 5 = ___	5 + 4 = ___
4.	5 + 8 = ___	5 + ___ = 9	5 − 5 = ___	5 + 6 = ___
5.	5 + 6 = ___	5 + ___ = 15	13 − 5 = ___	5 + 9 = ___
6.	5 + 3 = ___	5 + ___ = 10	8 − 5 = ___	5 + 5 = ___
7.	5 + 10 = ___	5 + ___ = 12	11 − 5 = ___	5 + 10 = ___
8.	5 + 2 = ___	5 + ___ = 6	14 − 5 = ___	5 + 3 = ___
9.	5 + 9 = ___	5 + ___ = 8	7 − 5 = ___	5 + 1 = ___
10.	5 + 7 = ___	5 + ___ = 14	12 − 5 = ___	5 + 8 = ___
11.	5 + 5 = ___	___ + 5 = 5	___ − 5 = 5	___ + 5 = 12
12.	3 + 5 = ___	___ + 5 = 11	___ − 5 = 9	___ + 5 = 7
13.	8 + 5 = ___	___ + 5 = 14	___ − 5 = 3	___ + 5 = 10
14.	4 + 5 = ___	___ + 5 = 12	___ − 5 = 10	5 + ___ = 9
15.	6 + 5 = ___	___ + 5 = 7	___ − 5 = 6	5 + ___ = 15
16.	9 + 5 = ___	___ + 5 = 15	___ − 5 = 4	___ − 5 = 6
17.	7 + 5 = ___	___ + 5 = 9	___ − 5 = 8	___ − 5 = 8
18.	0 + 5 = ___	___ + 5 = 13	___ − 5 = 0	___ − 5 = 2
19.	2 + 5 = ___	___ + 5 = 10	___ − 5 = 2	___ − 5 = 7
20.	10 + 5 = ___	___ + 5 = 8	___ − 5 = 7	___ − 5 = 0
	Score ___/20	Score ___/20	Score ___/20	Score ___/20

Week 5

6+, −6 Revision

Weekly Assessment ☹ ☐ 😐 ☐ ☺ ☐

Monday

Time allowed: 4:57 minutes

1.	6 + 10 = 16
2.	6 + 3 = 9
3.	6 + 5 = 11
4.	6 + 0 = 6
5.	6 + 8 = 14
6.	6 + 4 = 10
7.	6 + 6 = 12
8.	6 + 9 = 15
9.	6 + 2 = 8
10.	6 + 7 = 13
11.	9 + 6 = 15
12.	3 + 6 = 9
13.	6 + 6 = 12
14.	1 + 6 = 7
15.	4 + 6 = 10
16.	7 + 6 = 13
17.	2 + 6 = 8
18.	10 + 6 = 16
19.	8 + 6 = 14
20.	5 + 6 = 11

Score ____ / 20

Tuesday

Time allowed: 3:14 minutes

1.	6 + 6 = 12
2.	6 + 4 = 10
3.	6 + 0 = 6
4.	6 + 7 = 13
5.	6 + 9 = 15
6.	6 + 2 = 8
7.	6 + 5 = 11
8.	6 + 8 = 14
9.	6 + 3 = 9
10.	6 + 10 = 16
11.	6 + 6 = 12
12.	4 + 6 = 10
13.	9 + 6 = 15
14.	5 + 6 = 11
15.	1 + 6 = 7
16.	7 + 6 = 13
17.	3 + 6 = 9
18.	8 + 6 = 14
19.	10 + 6 = 16
20.	2 + 6 = 8

Score 20 / 20

Wednesday

Time allowed: minutes

1.	16 − 6 =
2.	12 − 6 =
3.	10 − 6 =
4.	8 − 6 =
5.	15 − 6 =
6.	11 − 6 =
7.	13 − 6 =
8.	9 − 6 =
9.	7 − 6 =
10.	14 − 6 =
11.	− 6 = 10
12.	− 6 = 2
13.	− 6 = 7
14.	− 6 = 3
15.	− 6 = 9
16.	− 6 = 5
17.	− 6 = 8
18.	− 6 = 0
19.	− 6 = 4
20.	− 6 = 6

Score ____ / 20

Thursday

Time allowed: minutes

1.	6 + 6 =
2.	6 + 3 =
3.	6 + 0 =
4.	6 + 5 =
5.	6 + 10 =
6.	6 + 7 =
7.	6 + 2 =
8.	6 + 8 =
9.	6 + 4 =
10.	6 + 9 =
11.	+ 6 = 11
12.	+ 6 = 15
13.	+ 6 = 13
14.	6 + = 9
15.	6 + = 14
16.	− 6 = 3
17.	− 6 = 4
18.	− 6 = 8
19.	− 6 = 6
20.	− 6 = 5

Score ____ / 20

Week 6

7+, −7 Revision

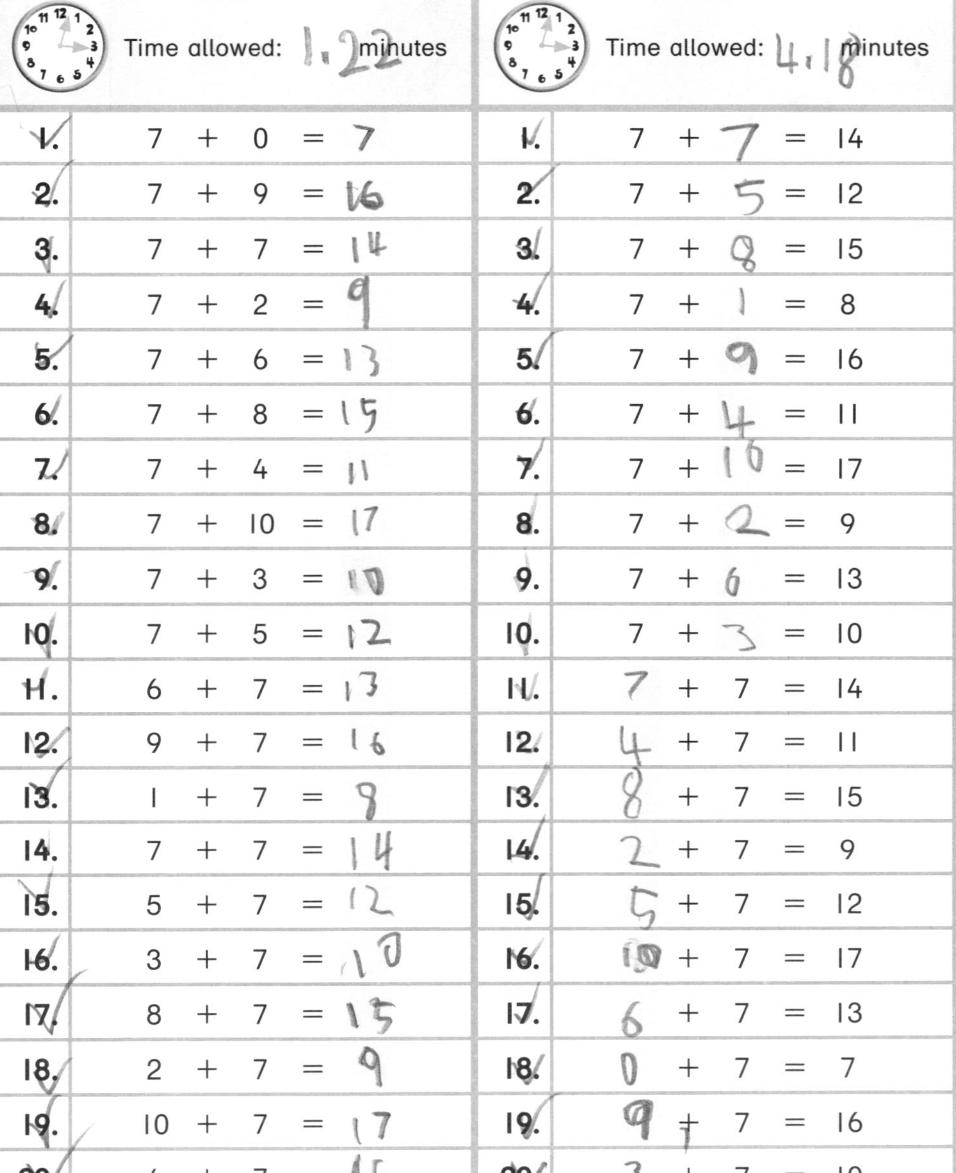

Monday

Time allowed: 1.22 minutes

1.	7 + 0 = 7
2.	7 + 9 = 16
3.	7 + 7 = 14
4.	7 + 2 = 9
5.	7 + 6 = 13
6.	7 + 8 = 15
7.	7 + 4 = 11
8.	7 + 10 = 17
9.	7 + 3 = 10
10.	7 + 5 = 12
11.	6 + 7 = 13
12.	9 + 7 = 16
13.	1 + 7 = 8
14.	7 + 7 = 14
15.	5 + 7 = 12
16.	3 + 7 = 10
17.	8 + 7 = 15
18.	2 + 7 = 9
19.	10 + 7 = 17
20.	4 + 7 = 11

Score 20 / 20

Tuesday

Time allowed: 4.18 minutes

1.	7 + 7 = 14
2.	7 + 5 = 12
3.	7 + 8 = 15
4.	7 + 1 = 8
5.	7 + 9 = 16
6.	7 + 4 = 11
7.	7 + 10 = 17
8.	7 + 2 = 9
9.	7 + 6 = 13
10.	7 + 3 = 10
11.	7 + 7 = 14
12.	4 + 7 = 11
13.	8 + 7 = 15
14.	2 + 7 = 9
15.	5 + 7 = 12
16.	10 + 7 = 17
17.	6 + 7 = 13
18.	0 + 7 = 7
19.	9 + 7 = 16
20.	3 + 7 = 10

Score 20 / 20

Wednesday

Time allowed: ___ minutes

1.	14 − 7 = 7
2.	10 − 7 = 3
3.	15 − 7 = 8
4.	12 − 7 = 5
5.	17 − 7 = 10
6.	13 − 7 = 6
7.	8 − 7 = 1
8.	11 − 7 = 4
9.	9 − 7 = 2
10.	16 − 7 = 9
11.	13 − 7 = 6
12.	10 − 7 = 3
13.	17 − 7 = 10
14.	12 − 7 = 5
15.	14 − 7 = 7
16.	___ − 7 = 0
17.	___ − 7 = 9
18.	___ − 7 = 4
19.	___ − 7 = 2
20.	___ − 7 = 8

Score ___ / 20

Thursday

Time allowed: 4;47 minutes

1.	7 + 6 = 13
2.	7 + 2 = 9
3.	7 + 5 = 12
4.	7 + 7 = 14
5.	7 + 9 = 16
6.	7 + 4 = 11
7.	7 + 10 = 17
8.	7 + 0 = 7
9.	7 + 3 = 10
10.	7 + 8 = 15
11.	3 + 7 = 10
12.	10 + 7 = 17
13.	5 + 7 = 12
14.	7 + 4 = 11
15.	7 + 7 = 14
16.	15 − 7 = 8
17.	8 − 7 = 1
18.	13 − 7 = 6
19.	11 − 7 = 4
20.	10 − 7 = 3

Score ___ / 20

Week 7

8+, –8 Revision

Weekly Assessment ☹ ☐ 😐 ☐ ☺ ☐

Monday

Time allowed: 25 minutes

1.	8 + 10 = 18
2.	8 + 8 = 16
3.	8 + 0 = 8
4.	8 + 3 = 11
5.	8 + 7 = 15
6.	8 + 5 = 13
7.	8 + 2 = 10
8.	8 + 9 = 17
9.	8 + 6 = 14
10.	8 + 4 = 12
11.	5 + 8 = 13
12.	7 + 8 = 15
13.	2 + 8 = 10
14.	6 + 8 = 14
15.	10 + 8 = 18
16.	3 + 8 = 11
17.	9 + 8 = 17
18.	4 + 8 = 12
19.	0 + 8 = 8
20.	8 + 8 = 16

Score 2 / 20

Tuesday

Time allowed: minutes

1.	8 + = 18
2.	8 + = 9
3.	8 + = 13
4.	8 + = 15
5.	8 + = 10
6.	8 + = 17
7.	8 + = 11
8.	8 + = 14
9.	8 + = 12
10.	8 + = 16
11.	+ 8 = 11
12.	+ 8 = 9
13.	+ 8 = 16
14.	+ 8 = 10
15.	+ 8 = 8
16.	+ 8 = 14
17.	+ 8 = 17
18.	+ 8 = 13
19.	+ 8 = 15
20.	+ 8 = 12

Score / 20

Wednesday

Time allowed: minutes

1.	18 – 8 =
2.	12 – 8 =
3.	9 – 8 =
4.	14 – 8 =
5.	17 – 8 =
6.	11 – 8 =
7.	15 – 8 =
8.	10 – 8 =
9.	13 – 8 =
10.	16 – 8 =
11.	– 8 = 10
12.	– 8 = 4
13.	– 8 = 8
14.	– 8 = 0
15.	– 8 = 5
16.	– 8 = 9
17.	– 8 = 2
18.	– 8 = 6
19.	– 8 = 3
20.	– 8 = 7

Score / 20

Thursday

Time allowed: minutes

1.	8 + 2 =
2.	8 + 10 =
3.	8 + 3 =
4.	8 + 9 =
5.	8 + 1 =
6.	8 + 5 =
7.	8 + 7 =
8.	8 + 4 =
9.	8 + 6 =
10.	8 + 8 =
11.	+ 8 = 14
12.	+ 8 = 18
13.	+ 8 = 12
14.	8 + = 16
15.	8 + = 10
16.	– 8 = 3
17.	– 8 = 9
18.	– 8 = 7
19.	– 8 = 10
20.	– 8 = 6

Score / 20

Week 8

9+, –9 Revision

Weekly Assessment ☹ ☐ 😐 ☐ ☺ ☐

Monday

Time allowed: 30 minutes

1.	9 + 0 = 9
2.	9 + 10 = 19
3.	9 + 5 = 14
4.	9 + 4 = 13
5.	9 + 9 = 18
6.	9 + 2 = 11
7.	9 + 7 = 16
8.	9 + 8 = 17
9.	9 + 6 = 15
10.	9 + 3 = 12
11.	5 + 9 = 14
12.	4 + 9 = 13
13.	7 + 9 = 16
14.	1 + 9 = 10
15.	10 + 9 = 19
16.	6 + 9 = 15
17.	9 + 9 = 18
18.	2 + 9 = 11
19.	8 + 9 = 17
20.	3 + 9 = 12

Score 20/20

Tuesday

Time allowed: 30 sec

1.	9 + 9 = 18
2.	9 + 7 = 16
3.	9 + 5 = 14
4.	9 + 3 = 12
5.	9 + 6 = 15
6.	9 + 4 = 13
7.	9 + 2 = 11
8.	9 + 0 = 9
9.	9 + 8 = 17
10.	9 + 1 = 10
11.	10 + 9 = 19
12.	3 + 9 = 12
13.	7 + 9 = 16
14.	9 + 9 = 18
15.	2 + 9 = 11
16.	4 + 9 = 13
17.	8 + 9 = 17
18.	5 + 9 = 14
19.	1 + 9 = 10
20.	6 + 9 = 15

Score 20/20

Wednesday

Time allowed: 3:49 minutes

1.	19 – 9 = 10
2.	14 – 9 = 5
3.	16 – 9 = 7
4.	9 – 9 = 0
5.	11 – 9 = 2
6.	17 – 9 = 8
7.	12 – 9 = 3
8.	15 – 9 = 6
9.	13 – 9 = 4
10.	18 – 9 = 9
11.	19 – 9 = 10
12.	15 – 9 = 6
13.	11 – 9 = 2
14.	16 – 9 = 7
15.	13 – 9 = 4
16.	18 – 9 = 9
17.	10 – 9 = 1
18.	14 – 9 = 5
19.	12 – 9 = 3
20.	17 – 9 = 8

Score 20/20

Thursday

Time allowed: 1:48 minutes

1.	9 + 10 = 19
2.	9 + 2 = 11
3.	9 + 0 = 9
4.	9 + 3 = 12
5.	9 + 8 = 17
6.	9 + 5 = 14
7.	9 + 9 = 18
8.	9 + 6 = 15
9.	9 + 4 = 13
10.	9 + 10 = 19
11.	5 + 9 = 14
12.	10 + 9 = 19
13.	1 + 9 = 10
14.	9 + 3 = 12
15.	9 + 7 = 16
16.	18 – 9 = 9
17.	15 – 9 = 6
18.	9 – 9 = 0
19.	12 – 9 = 3
20.	14 – 9 = 5

Score 20/20

Week 9

10+, – 10 Revision

Weekly Assessment ☹ ☐ 😐 ☐ ☺ ☐

Monday

Time allowed: 30 sec minutes

1.	10 + 10 = 20
2.	10 + 2 = 12
3.	10 + 6 = 16
4.	10 + 3 = 13
5.	10 + 5 = 15
6.	10 + 7 = 17
7.	10 + 9 = 19
8.	10 + 4 = 14
9.	10 + 1 = 11
10.	10 + 8 = 18
11.	4 + 10 = 14
12.	2 + 10 = 12
13.	7 + 10 = 17
14.	0 + 10 = 10
15.	6 + 10 = 16
16.	1 + 10 = 11
17.	3 + 10 = 13
18.	9 + 10 = 19
19.	5 + 10 = 15
20.	8 + 10 = 18

Score 20 / 20

Tuesday

Time allowed: minutes

1.	10 + = 17
2.	10 + = 14
3.	10 + = 20
4.	10 + = 12
5.	10 + = 16
6.	10 + = 13
7.	10 + = 15
8.	10 + = 19
9.	10 + = 10
10.	10 + = 18
11.	+ 10 = 14
12.	+ 10 = 18
13.	+ 10 = 15
14.	+ 10 = 19
15.	+ 10 = 17
16.	+ 10 = 11
17.	+ 10 = 16
18.	+ 10 = 13
19.	+ 10 = 20
20.	+ 10 = 12

Score ____ / 20

Wednesday

Time allowed: 30 sec minutes

1.	20 – 10 = 10
2.	12 – 10 = 2
3.	14 – 10 = 4
4.	19 – 10 = 9
5.	10 – 10 = 0
6.	15 – 10 = 5
7.	18 – 10 = 8
8.	16 – 10 = 6
9.	13 – 10 = 3
10.	17 – 10 = 7
11.	16 – 10 = 6
12.	13 – 10 = 3
13.	10 – 10 = 10
14.	15 – 10 = 5
15.	17 – 10 = 7
16.	12 – 10 = 2
17.	19 – 10 = 9
18.	11 – 10 = 1
19.	14 – 10 = 4
20.	18 – 10 = 8

Score ____ / 20

Thursday

Time allowed: minutes

1.	10 + 8 = 18
2.	10 + 2 = 12
3.	10 + 4 = 14
4.	10 + 7 = 17
5.	10 + 5 = 15
6.	10 + 9 = 19
7.	10 + 6 = 16
8.	10 + 10 = 20
9.	10 + 3 = 13
10.	10 + 0 = 10
11.	7 + 10 = 17
12.	5 + 10 = 15
13.	6 + 10 = 16
14.	10 + 9 = 19
15.	10 + 1 = 11
16.	17 – 10 = 7
17.	14 – 10 = 4
18.	18 – 10 = 8
19.	19 – 10 = 9
20.	15 – 10 = 5

Score ____ / 20

Week 10

Look Back

Weekly Assessment ☹ ☐ 😐 ☐ ☺ ☐

#	Monday	Tuesday	Wednesday	Thursday
	Time allowed: ___ minutes	Time allowed: ___ minutes	Time allowed: ___ minutes	Time allowed: ___ minutes
1.	2 + 6 = ___	5 + ___ = 12	7 − 2 = ___	2 + 7 = ___
2.	3 + 8 = ___	6 + ___ = 14	10 − 2 = ___	3 + 0 = ___
3.	4 + 3 = ___	7 + ___ = 17	9 − 2 = ___	4 + 5 = ___
4.	9 + 8 = ___	8 + ___ = 12	3 − 3 = ___	5 + 8 = ___
5.	2 + 5 = ___	9 + ___ = 16	8 − 3 = ___	6 + 9 = ___
6.	3 + 9 = ___	10 + ___ = 18	10 − 3 = ___	7 + 4 = ___
7.	4 + 4 = ___	5 + ___ = 11	6 − 4 = ___	8 + 3 = ___
8.	5 + 2 = ___	5 + ___ = 8	13 − 4 = ___	9 + 5 = ___
9.	6 + 10 = ___	4 + ___ = 12	12 − 5 = ___	10 + 6 = ___
10.	2 + 9 = ___	6 + ___ = 15	14 − 5 = ___	10 + 10 = ___
11.	3 + 7 = ___	___ + 6 = 9	___ − 5 = 6	___ + 2 = 11
12.	4 + 5 = ___	___ + 4 = 13	___ − 6 = 8	___ + 3 = 7
13.	4 + 6 = ___	___ + 5 = 15	___ − 6 = 4	___ + 5 = 13
14.	6 + 5 = ___	___ + 8 = 17	___ − 7 = 7	6 + ___ = 15
15.	5 + 10 = ___	___ + 9 = 14	___ − 8 = 10	8 + ___ = 8
16.	4 + 9 = ___	___ + 6 = 16	___ − 8 = 6	___ − 7 = 5
17.	6 + 8 = ___	___ + 5 = 7	___ − 9 = 5	___ − 8 = 3
18.	5 + 7 = ___	___ + 4 = 11	___ − 9 = 7	___ − 5 = 8
19.	3 + 8 = ___	___ + 3 = 12	___ − 10 = 10	___ − 4 = 9
20.	2 + 6 = ___	___ + 2 = 11	___ − 10 = 0	___ − 6 = 7
	Score ___ / 20	Score ___ / 20	Score ___ / 20	Score ___ / 20

Check-up 1

A		B		C		D	
1.	2 + 5 =	1.	4 + = 10	1.	9 − 2 =	1.	− 3 = 6
2.	4 + 6 =	2.	5 + = 11	2.	12 − 4 =	2.	− 2 = 9
3.	3 + 8 =	3.	2 + = 9	3.	10 − 3 =	3.	− 5 = 4
4.	5 + 7 =	4.	10 + = 14	4.	16 − 10 =	4.	− 6 = 8
5.	10 + 2 =	5.	3 + = 10	5.	11 − 5 =	5.	− 4 = 7
6.	6 + 5 =	6.	8 + = 14	6.	15 − 8 =	6.	− 8 = 5
7.	8 + 7 =	7.	6 + = 15	7.	13 − 6 =	7.	− 7 = 9
8.	8 + 9 =	8.	7 + = 12	8.	10 − 7 =	8.	− 9 = 8
9.	7 + 6 =	9.	+ 9 = 16	9.	17 − 9 =	9.	− 7 = 8
10.	9 + 4 =	10.	7 + = 15	10.	14 − 6 =	10.	− 6 = 7

Score ____ / 40

How did you do? ☹ ☐ 😐 ☐ ☺ ☐

Week 11

Multiplication × 2

Weekly Assessment ☹ ☐ 😐 ☐ ☺ ☐

	Monday	Tuesday	Wednesday	Thursday
Time allowed:	33 ~~minutes~~ sec	22 ~~minutes~~ sec	115 minutes	20 minutes
1.	1 × 2 = 2	4 × 2 = 8	10 × 2 = 20	10 × 2 = 20
2.	2 × 2 = 4	0 × 2 = 0	8 × 2 = 16	4 × 2 = 8
3.	3 × 2 = 6	3 × 2 = 6	3 × 2 = 6	0 × 2 = 0
4.	4 × 2 = 8	7 × 2 = 14	7 × 2 = 14	9 × 2 = 18
5.	5 × 2 = 10	5 × 2 = 10	4 × 2 = 8	3 × 2 = 6
6.	6 × 2 = 12	2 × 2 = 4	10 × 2 = 20	6 × 2 = 12
7.	7 × 2 = 14	9 × 2 = 18	2 × 2 = 4	8 × 2 = 16
8.	8 × 2 = 16	6 × 2 = 12	9 × 2 = 18	5 × 2 = 10
9.	9 × 2 = 18	1 × 2 = 2	5 × 2 = 10	2 × 2 = 4
10.	10 × 2 = 20	8 × 2 = 16	1 × 2 = 2	7 × 2 = 14
11.	7 × 2 = 14	6 × 2 = 12	8 × 2 = 16	9 × 2 = 18
12.	8 × 2 = 16	4 × 2 = 8	5 × 2 = 10	4 × 2 = 8
13.	1 × 2 = 2	9 × 2 = 18	10 × 2 = 20	8 × 2 = 16
14.	6 × 2 = 12	3 × 2 = 6	0 × 2 = 0	1 × 2 = 2
15.	9 × 2 = 18	10 × 2 = 20	2 × 2 = 4	7 × 2 = 14
16.	2 × 2 = 4	2 × 2 = 4	7 × 2 = 14	3 × 2 = 6
17.	5 × 2 = 10	7 × 2 = 14	4 × 2 = 8	6 × 2 = 12
18.	3 × 2 = 6	0 × 2 = 0	9 × 2 = 18	10 × 2 = 20
19.	10 × 2 = 20	5 × 2 = 10	6 × 2 = 12	2 × 2 = 4
20.	4 × 2 = 8	8 × 2 = 16	3 × 2 = 6	5 × 2 = 10
Score	20/20	20/20	20/20	20/20

Week 12

Multiplication ×4

Weekly Assessment ☹ ☐ 😐 ☐ ☺ ☐

Monday

Time allowed: minutes

1.	1	×	4	=	4
2.	2	×	4	=	8
3.	3	×	4	=	
4.	4	×	4	=	
5.	5	×	4	=	
6.	6	×	4	=	
7.	7	×	4	=	
8.	8	×	4	=	
9.	9	×	4	=	
10.	10	×	4	=	
11.	5	×	4	=	
12.	7	×	4	=	
13.	3	×	4	=	
14.	6	×	4	=	
15.	4	×	4	=	
16.	9	×	4	=	
17.	2	×	4	=	
18.	1	×	4	=	
19.	8	×	4	=	
20.	0	×	4	=	

Score ____ / 20

Tuesday

Time allowed: minutes

1.	10	×	4	=	
2.	0	×	4	=	
3.	8	×	4	=	
4.	2	×	4	=	
5.	9	×	4	=	
6.	5	×	4	=	
7.	3	×	4	=	
8.	6	×	4	=	
9.	7	×	4	=	
10.	4	×	4	=	
11.	0	×	4	=	
12.	6	×	4	=	
13.	4	×	4	=	
14.	1	×	4	=	
15.	10	×	4	=	
16.	8	×	4	=	
17.	3	×	4	=	
18.	9	×	4	=	
19.	7	×	4	=	
20.	5	×	4	=	

Score ____ / 20

Wednesday

Time allowed: minutes

1.	8	×	4	=	32
2.	0	×	4	=	0
3.	10	×	4	=	40
4.	3	×	4	=	12
5.	5	×	4	=	20
6.	2	×	4	=	8
7.	4	×	4	=	16
8.	9	×	4	=	36
9.	6	×	4	=	24
10.	7	×	4	=	28
11.	1	×	4	=	4
12.	5	×	4	=	20
13.	7	×	4	=	28
14.	8	×	4	=	32
15.	4	×	4	=	16
16.	6	×	4	=	24
17.	10	×	4	=	40
18.	3	×	4	=	12
19.	9	×	4	=	36
20.	2	×	4	=	8

Score ____ / 20

Thursday

Time allowed: minutes

1.	2	×	4	=	
2.	6	×	4	=	
3.	9	×	4	=	
4.	5	×	4	=	
5.	8	×	4	=	
6.	4	×	4	=	
7.	7	×	4	=	
8.	10	×	4	=	
9.	3	×	4	=	
10.	1	×	4	=	
11.	6	×	4	=	
12.	8	×	4	=	
13.	3	×	4	=	
14.	7	×	4	=	
15.	10	×	4	=	
16.	2	×	4	=	
17.	9	×	4	=	
18.	4	×	4	=	
19.	0	×	4	=	
20.	5	×	4	=	

Score ____ / 20

Week 13

Multiplication ×8

Weekly Assessment ☹ ☐ 😐 ☐ ☺ ☐

Monday

Time allowed: minutes

1.	1 × 8 =
2.	2 × 8 =
3.	3 × 8 =
4.	4 × 8 =
5.	5 × 8 =
6.	6 × 8 =
7.	7 × 8 =
8.	8 × 8 =
9.	9 × 8 =
10.	10 × 8 =
11.	7 × 8 =
12.	2 × 8 =
13.	8 × 8 =
14.	3 × 8 =
15.	9 × 8 =
16.	4 × 8 =
17.	10 × 8 =
18.	5 × 8 =
19.	0 × 8 =
20.	6 × 8 =

Score ___ / 20

Tuesday

Time allowed: minutes

1.	10 × 8 =
2.	7 × 8 =
3.	2 × 8 =
4.	8 × 8 =
5.	0 × 8 =
6.	4 × 8 =
7.	9 × 8 =
8.	5 × 8 =
9.	3 × 8 =
10.	6 × 8 =
11.	1 × 8 =
12.	7 × 8 =
13.	5 × 8 =
14.	9 × 8 =
15.	6 × 8 =
16.	2 × 8 =
17.	4 × 8 =
18.	10 × 8 =
19.	8 × 8 =
20.	3 × 8 =

Score ___ / 20

Wednesday

Time allowed: minutes

1.	3 × 8 =
2.	9 × 8 =
3.	7 × 8 =
4.	10 × 8 =
5.	4 × 8 =
6.	8 × 8 =
7.	5 × 8 =
8.	2 × 8 =
9.	6 × 8 =
10.	0 × 8 =
11.	3 × 8 =
12.	10 × 8 =
13.	9 × 8 =
14.	4 × 8 =
15.	8 × 8 =
16.	5 × 8 =
17.	2 × 8 =
18.	6 × 8 =
19.	1 × 8 =
20.	7 × 8 =

Score ___ / 20

Thursday

Time allowed: minutes

1.	5 × 8 =
2.	10 × 8 =
3.	0 × 8 =
4.	9 × 8 =
5.	7 × 8 =
6.	3 × 8 =
7.	6 × 8 =
8.	4 × 8 =
9.	2 × 8 =
10.	8 × 8 =
11.	6 × 8 =
12.	4 × 8 =
13.	7 × 8 =
14.	5 × 8 =
15.	2 × 8 =
16.	8 × 8 =
17.	0 × 8 =
18.	9 × 8 =
19.	3 × 8 =
20.	10 × 8 =

Score ___ / 20

Week 14

Multiplication ×5

Weekly Assessment ☹ ☐ 😐 ☐ ☺ ☐

Monday		Tuesday		Wednesday		Thursday	
Time allowed: minutes		Time allowed: minutes		Time allowed: minutes		Time allowed: minutes	
1.	1 × 5 =	1.	10 × 5 =	1.	7 × 5 =	1.	4 × 5 =
2.	2 × 5 =	2.	7 × 5 =	2.	1 × 5 =	2.	9 × 5 =
3.	3 × 5 =	3.	0 × 5 =	3.	4 × 5 =	3.	2 × 5 =
4.	4 × 5 =	4.	9 × 5 =	4.	6 × 5 =	4.	5 × 5 =
5.	5 × 5 =	5.	3 × 5 =	5.	10 × 5 =	5.	3 × 5 =
6.	6 × 5 =	6.	8 × 5 =	6.	2 × 5 =	6.	7 × 5 =
7.	7 × 5 =	7.	4 × 5 =	7.	5 × 5 =	7.	10 × 5 =
8.	8 × 5 =	8.	6 × 5 =	8.	3 × 5 =	8.	6 × 5 =
9.	9 × 5 =	9.	2 × 5 =	9.	8 × 5 =	9.	1 × 5 =
10.	10 × 5 =	10.	5 × 5 =	10.	9 × 5 =	10.	8 × 5 =
11.	5 × 5 =	11.	7 × 5 =	11.	6 × 5 =	11.	3 × 5 =
12.	7 × 5 =	12.	4 × 5 =	12.	3 × 5 =	12.	0 × 5 =
13.	2 × 5 =	13.	9 × 5 =	13.	8 × 5 =	13.	6 × 5 =
14.	9 × 5 =	14.	3 × 5 =	14.	5 × 5 =	14.	2 × 5 =
15.	6 × 5 =	15.	8 × 5 =	15.	9 × 5 =	15.	1 × 5 =
16.	0 × 5 =	16.	10 × 5 =	16.	2 × 5 =	16.	5 × 5 =
17.	3 × 5 =	17.	5 × 5 =	17.	7 × 5 =	17.	9 × 5 =
18.	10 × 5 =	18.	2 × 5 =	18.	4 × 5 =	18.	7 × 5 =
19.	4 × 5 =	19.	6 × 5 =	19.	10 × 5 =	19.	8 × 5 =
20.	8 × 5 =	20.	1 × 5 =	20.	0 × 5 =	20.	4 × 5 =
Score ___ / 20		Score ___ / 20		Score ___ / 20		Score ___ / 20	

Week 15

Multiplication × 10

Weekly Assessment ☹ ☐ 😐 ☐ 🙂 ☐

Monday

Time allowed: minutes

1. 1 × 10 =
2. 2 × 10 =
3. 3 × 10 =
4. 4 × 10 =
5. 5 × 10 =
6. 6 × 10 =
7. 7 × 10 =
8. 8 × 10 =
9. 9 × 10 =
10. 10 × 10 =
11. 3 × 10 =
12. 9 × 10 =
13. 4 × 10 =
14. 10 × 10 =
15. 5 × 10 =
16. 2 × 10 =
17. 8 × 10 =
18. 6 × 10 =
19. 1 × 10 =
20. 7 × 10 =

Score ____ / 20

Tuesday

Time allowed: minutes

1. 10 × 10 =
2. 0 × 10 =
3. 6 × 10 =
4. 9 × 10 =
5. 3 × 10 =
6. 8 × 10 =
7. 5 × 10 =
8. 2 × 10 =
9. 7 × 10 =
10. 4 × 10 =
11. 9 × 10 =
12. 4 × 10 =
13. 1 × 10 =
14. 6 × 10 =
15. 7 × 10 =
16. 5 × 10 =
17. 3 × 10 =
18. 10 × 10 =
19. 8 × 10 =
20. 2 × 10 =

Score ____ / 20

Wednesday

Time allowed: minutes

1. 5 × 10 =
2. 8 × 10 =
3. 3 × 10 =
4. 2 × 10 =
5. 7 × 10 =
6. 4 × 10 =
7. 6 × 10 =
8. 0 × 10 =
9. 10 × 10 =
10. 9 × 10 =
11. 1 × 10 =
12. 5 × 10 =
13. 7 × 10 =
14. 2 × 10 =
15. 8 × 10 =
16. 6 × 10 =
17. 9 × 10 =
18. 4 × 10 =
19. 3 × 10 =
20. 10 × 10 =

Score ____ / 20

Thursday

Time allowed: minutes

1. 4 × 10 =
2. 8 × 10 =
3. 10 × 10 =
4. 5 × 10 =
5. 2 × 10 =
6. 7 × 10 =
7. 9 × 10 =
8. 3 × 10 =
9. 6 × 10 =
10. 0 × 10 =
11. 4 × 10 =
12. 3 × 10 =
13. 2 × 10 =
14. 9 × 10 =
15. 6 × 10 =
16. 8 × 10 =
17. 1 × 10 =
18. 7 × 10 =
19. 5 × 10 =
20. 10 × 10 =

Score ____ / 20

Check-up 2

A		B		C		D	
1.	5 × 2 =	1.	3 × 4 =	1.	4 × 8 =	1.	3 × 5 =
2.	2 × 8 =	2.	4 × 5 =	2.	2 × 2 =	2.	8 × 10 =
3.	3 × 10 =	3.	3 × 2 =	3.	5 × 5 =	3.	7 × 2 =
4.	4 × 2 =	4.	5 × 8 =	4.	7 × 4 =	4.	6 × 4 =
5.	8 × 4 =	5.	9 × 4 =	5.	7 × 10 =	5.	9 × 8 =
6.	6 × 8 =	6.	10 × 10 =	6.	6 × 5 =	6.	5 × 0 =
7.	2 × 4 =	7.	6 × 2 =	7.	5 × 4 =	7.	9 × 2 =
8.	7 × 5 =	8.	4 × 10 =	8.	7 × 8 =	8.	10 × 5 =
9.	5 × 10 =	9.	8 × 8 =	9.	9 × 5 =	9.	4 × 4 =
10.	1 × 5 =	10.	8 × 5 =	10.	8 × 2 =	10.	3 × 8 =

Score ____ / 40

How did you do?

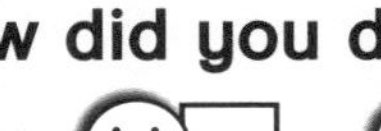

Week 16

Multiplication ×3

Weekly Assessment ☹ ☐ 😐 ☐ ☺ ☐

Monday

Time allowed: ____ minutes

1.	1 × 3 =
2.	2 × 3 =
3.	3 × 3 =
4.	4 × 3 =
5.	5 × 3 =
6.	6 × 3 =
7.	7 × 3 =
8.	8 × 3 =
9.	9 × 3 =
10.	10 × 3 =
11.	5 × 3 =
12.	7 × 3 =
13.	2 × 3 =
14.	6 × 3 =
15.	0 × 3 =
16.	9 × 3 =
17.	8 × 3 =
18.	4 × 3 =
19.	10 × 3 =
20.	3 × 3 =

Score ____ / 20

Tuesday

Time allowed: ____ minutes

1.	10 × 3 =
2.	6 × 3 =
3.	0 × 3 =
4.	7 × 3 =
5.	3 × 3 =
6.	4 × 3 =
7.	9 × 3 =
8.	5 × 3 =
9.	2 × 3 =
10.	8 × 3 =
11.	1 × 3 =
12.	5 × 3 =
13.	3 × 3 =
14.	9 × 3 =
15.	2 × 3 =
16.	10 × 3 =
17.	4 × 3 =
18.	7 × 3 =
19.	6 × 3 =
20.	8 × 3 =

Score ____ / 20

Wednesday

Time allowed: ____ minutes

1.	3 × 3 =
2.	9 × 3 =
3.	5 × 3 =
4.	4 × 3 =
5.	6 × 3 =
6.	10 × 3 =
7.	0 × 3 =
8.	8 × 3 =
9.	2 × 3 =
10.	7 × 3 =
11.	10 × 3 =
12.	0 × 3 =
13.	5 × 3 =
14.	8 × 3 =
15.	1 × 3 =
16.	6 × 3 =
17.	3 × 3 =
18.	7 × 3 =
19.	9 × 3 =
20.	4 × 3 =

Score ____ / 20

Thursday

Time allowed: ____ minutes

1.	4 × 3 =
2.	9 × 3 =
3.	5 × 3 =
4.	0 × 3 =
5.	10 × 3 =
6.	3 × 3 =
7.	7 × 3 =
8.	2 × 3 =
9.	8 × 3 =
10.	6 × 3 =
11.	9 × 3 =
12.	4 × 3 =
13.	1 × 3 =
14.	10 × 3 =
15.	8 × 3 =
16.	7 × 3 =
17.	6 × 3 =
18.	3 × 3 =
19.	5 × 3 =
20.	2 × 3 =

Score ____ / 20

Week 17

Multiplication ×6

Weekly Assessment ☹ ☐ 😐 ☐ ☺ ☐

Monday

Time allowed: 1½ minutes

1.	1	×	6	=	6
2.	2	×	6	=	12
3.	3	×	6	=	18
4.	4	×	6	=	24
5.	5	×	6	=	30
6.	6	×	6	=	36
7.	7	×	6	=	42
8.	8	×	6	=	48
9.	9	×	6	=	54
10.	10	×	6	=	60
11.	4	×	6	=	24
12.	7	×	6	=	42
13.	3	×	6	=	18
14.	8	×	6	=	48
15.	0	×	6	=	0
16.	9	×	6	=	54
17.	5	×	6	=	30
18.	10	×	6	=	60
19.	2	×	6	=	12
20.	6	×	6	=	36

Score ___ / 20

Tuesday

Time allowed: minutes

1.	10	×	6	=	60
2.	4	×	6	=	24
3.	9	×	6	=	54
4.	3	×	6	=	18
5.	8	×	6	=	48
6.	0	×	6	=	0
7.	5	×	6	=	30
8.	7	×	6	=	42
9.	2	×	6	=	12
10.	6	×	6	=	36
11.	1	×	6	=	6
12.	8	×	6	=	48
13.	5	×	6	=	30
14.	9	×	6	=	54
15.	3	×	6	=	18
16.	6	×	6	=	36
17.	2	×	6	=	12
18.	7	×	6	=	42
19.	10	×	6	=	60
20.	4	×	6	=	24

Score 20 / 20

Wednesday

Time allowed: minutes

1.	5	×	6	=	30
2.	9	×	6	=	54
3.	2	×	6	=	12
4.	0	×	6	=	0
5.	6	×	6	=	38
6.	10	×	6	=	60
7.	7	×	6	=	42
8.	3	×	6	=	18
9.	4	×	6	=	24
10.	8	×	6	=	48
11.	6	×	6	=	36
12.	1	×	6	=	6
13.	10	×	6	=	60
14.	5	×	6	=	30
15.	7	×	6	=	42
16.	2	×	6	=	12
17.	4	×	6	=	24
18.	8	×	6	=	48
19.	3	×	6	=	18
20.	9	×	6	=	54

Score ___ / 20

Thursday

Time allowed: minutes

1.	3	×	6	=	
2.	5	×	6	=	
3.	10	×	6	=	
4.	8	×	6	=	
5.	4	×	6	=	
6.	7	×	6	=	
7.	0	×	6	=	
8.	2	×	6	=	
9.	6	×	6	=	
10.	9	×	6	=	
11.	0	×	6	=	
12.	4	×	6	=	
13.	8	×	6	=	
14.	3	×	6	=	
15.	9	×	6	=	
16.	1	×	6	=	
17.	6	×	6	=	
18.	5	×	6	=	
19.	7	×	6	=	
20.	2	×	6	=	

Score ___ / 20

Week 18

Multiplication ×9

Weekly Assessment

	Monday	Tuesday	Wednesday	Thursday
	Time allowed: minutes	Time allowed: minutes	Time allowed: minutes	Time allowed: minutes
1.	1 × 9 =	10 × 9 =	5 × 9 =	3 × 9 =
2.	2 × 9 =	7 × 9 =	0 × 9 =	4 × 9 =
3.	3 × 9 =	0 × 9 =	9 × 9 =	10 × 9 =
4.	4 × 9 =	8 × 9 =	6 × 9 =	2 × 9 =
5.	5 × 9 =	3 × 9 =	10 × 9 =	9 × 9 =
6.	6 × 9 =	5 × 9 =	8 × 9 =	0 × 9 =
7.	7 × 9 =	9 × 9 =	4 × 9 =	8 × 9 =
8.	8 × 9 =	6 × 9 =	2 × 9 =	7 × 9 =
9.	9 × 9 =	2 × 9 =	3 × 9 =	6 × 9 =
10.	10 × 9 =	4 × 9 =	7 × 9 =	5 × 9 =
11.	1 × 9 =	5 × 9 =	0 × 9 =	4 × 9 =
12.	7 × 9 =	8 × 9 =	6 × 9 =	9 × 9 =
13.	0 × 9 =	4 × 9 =	2 × 9 =	3 × 9 =
14.	9 × 9 =	6 × 9 =	10 × 9 =	7 × 9 =
15.	6 × 9 =	3 × 9 =	5 × 9 =	2 × 9 =
16.	2 × 9 =	9 × 9 =	7 × 9 =	10 × 9 =
17.	8 × 9 =	2 × 9 =	4 × 9 =	6 × 9 =
18.	4 × 9 =	7 × 9 =	9 × 9 =	0 × 9 =
19.	5 × 9 =	1 × 9 =	3 × 9 =	8 × 9 =
20.	3 × 9 =	0 × 9 =	8 × 9 =	5 × 9 =
	Score ___ / 20	Score ___ / 20	Score ___ / 20	Score ___ / 20

Week 19

Multiplication ×7

Weekly Assessment ☹ ☐ 😐 ☐ ☺ ☐

Monday

Time allowed: minutes

1.	1 × 7 =
2.	2 × 7 =
3.	3 × 7 =
4.	4 × 7 =
5.	5 × 7 =
6.	6 × 7 =
7.	7 × 7 =
8.	8 × 7 =
9.	9 × 7 =
10.	10 × 7 =
11.	4 × 7 =
12.	6 × 7 =
13.	0 × 7 =
14.	7 × 7 =
15.	5 × 7 =
16.	8 × 7 =
17.	2 × 7 =
18.	9 × 7 =
19.	3 × 7 =
20.	10 × 7 =

Score ___ / 20

Tuesday

Time allowed: minutes

1.	10 × 7 =
2.	0 × 7 =
3.	9 × 7 =
4.	7 × 7 =
5.	1 × 7 =
6.	4 × 7 =
7.	8 × 7 =
8.	6 × 7 =
9.	2 × 7 =
10.	5 × 7 =
11.	3 × 7 =
12.	8 × 7 =
13.	4 × 7 =
14.	6 × 7 =
15.	3 × 7 =
16.	7 × 7 =
17.	10 × 7 =
18.	2 × 7 =
19.	5 × 7 =
20.	9 × 7 =

Score ___ / 20

Wednesday

Time allowed: minutes

1.	8 × 7 =
2.	3 × 7 =
3.	10 × 7 =
4.	6 × 7 =
5.	2 × 7 =
6.	9 × 7 =
7.	0 × 7 =
8.	5 × 7 =
9.	7 × 7 =
10.	4 × 7 =
11.	2 × 7 =
12.	1 × 7 =
13.	7 × 7 =
14.	9 × 7 =
15.	5 × 7 =
16.	6 × 7 =
17.	4 × 7 =
18.	10 × 7 =
19.	8 × 7 =
20.	3 × 7 =

Score ___ / 20

Thursday

Time allowed: minutes

1.	0 × 7 =
2.	4 × 7 =
3.	2 × 7 =
4.	3 × 7 =
5.	7 × 7 =
6.	5 × 7 =
7.	1 × 7 =
8.	10 × 7 =
9.	6 × 7 =
10.	8 × 7 =
11.	9 × 7 =
12.	2 × 7 =
13.	4 × 7 =
14.	3 × 7 =
15.	6 × 7 =
16.	0 × 7 =
17.	5 × 7 =
18.	7 × 7 =
19.	10 × 7 =
20.	8 × 7 =

Score ___ / 20

Week 20 — Look Back

Weekly Assessment ☹ ☐ 😐 ☐ ☺ ☐

Monday

Time allowed: minutes

1.	9 × 2 =
2.	10 × 4 =
3.	5 × 8 =
4.	10 × 2 =
5.	5 × 4 =
6.	10 × 8 =
7.	8 × 2 =
8.	9 × 4 =
9.	3 × 8 =
10.	7 × 2 =
11.	6 × 8 =
12.	8 × 4 =
13.	7 × 8 =
14.	6 × 4 =
15.	5 × 2 =
16.	8 × 8 =
17.	7 × 4 =
18.	9 × 8 =
19.	4 × 8 =
20.	6 × 8 =

Score ___ / 20

Tuesday

Time allowed: minutes

1.	9 × 5 =
2.	0 × 5 =
3.	10 × 10 =
4.	5 × 5 =
5.	4 × 10 =
6.	10 × 5 =
7.	1 × 5 =
8.	4 × 5 =
9.	6 × 5 =
10.	0 × 10 =
11.	6 × 10 =
12.	9 × 10 =
13.	1 × 10 =
14.	3 × 5 =
15.	8 × 5 =
16.	7 × 10 =
17.	2 × 5 =
18.	3 × 10 =
19.	7 × 5 =
20.	8 × 10 =

Score ___ / 20

Wednesday

Time allowed: minutes

1.	3 × 3 =
2.	5 × 3 =
3.	6 × 6 =
4.	8 × 9 =
5.	9 × 3 =
6.	4 × 3 =
7.	5 × 6 =
8.	7 × 9 =
9.	8 × 3 =
10.	7 × 6 =
11.	4 × 9 =
12.	2 × 3 =
13.	6 × 3 =
14.	9 × 9 =
15.	8 × 6 =
16.	0 × 3 =
17.	5 × 9 =
18.	7 × 3 =
19.	6 × 9 =
20.	3 × 9 =

Score ___ / 20

Thursday

Time allowed: minutes

1.	6 × 7 =
2.	8 × 7 =
3.	5 × 7 =
4.	2 × 7 =
5.	9 × 7 =
6.	0 × 7 =
7.	3 × 7 =
8.	10 × 7 =
9.	7 × 7 =
10.	4 × 7 =
11.	7 × 5 =
12.	7 × 1 =
13.	7 × 6 =
14.	7 × 4 =
15.	7 × 2 =
16.	7 × 9 =
17.	7 × 6 =
18.	7 × 8 =
19.	7 × 3 =
20.	7 × 7 =

Score ___ / 20

Check-up 3

	A		B		C		D
1.	2 × 3 =	1.	1 × 9 =	1.	10 × 7 =	1.	0 × 6 =
2.	3 × 6 =	2.	3 × 3 =	2.	10 × 10 =	2.	8 × 3 =
3.	4 × 3 =	3.	4 × 9 =	3.	5 × 7 =	3.	7 × 6 =
4.	0 × 9 =	4.	6 × 3 =	4.	5 × 6 =	4.	8 × 8 =
5.	2 × 6 =	5.	3 × 7 =	5.	7 × 3 =	5.	9 × 3 =
6.	3 × 9 =	6.	4 × 6 =	6.	1 × 7 =	6.	7 × 9 =
7.	2 × 7 =	7.	5 × 9 =	7.	6 × 9 =	7.	7 × 7 =
8.	5 × 3 =	8.	6 × 6 =	8.	3 × 3 =	8.	9 × 6 =
9.	4 × 7 =	9.	0 × 7 =	9.	8 × 6 =	9.	8 × 9 =
10.	2 × 9 =	10.	8 × 7 =	10.	9 × 9 =	10.	6 × 7 =

Score ____ / 40

How did you do?

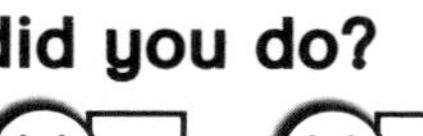

Week 21

Multiplication and Division ×2, ÷2

Weekly Assessment ☹ ☐ 😐 ☐ ☺ ☐

Monday

Time allowed: minutes

1.	10 × 2 =
2.	4 × 2 =
3.	6 × 2 =
4.	0 × 2 =
5.	5 × 2 =
6.	9 × 2 =
7.	3 × 2 =
8.	7 × 2 =
9.	2 × 2 =
10.	8 × 2 =
11.	4 × 2 =
12.	10 × 2 =
13.	1 × 2 =
14.	7 × 2 =
15.	5 × 2 =
16.	2 × 2 =
17.	9 × 2 =
18.	6 × 2 =
19.	8 × 2 =
20.	3 × 2 =

Score ____ / 20

Tuesday

Time allowed: minutes

1.	× 2 = 20
2.	× 2 = 14
3.	× 2 = 0
4.	× 2 = 12
5.	× 2 = 6
6.	× 2 = 16
7.	× 2 = 8
8.	× 2 = 10
9.	× 2 = 4
10.	× 2 = 18
11.	× 2 = 12
12.	× 2 = 16
13.	× 2 = 0
14.	× 2 = 14
15.	× 2 = 8
16.	× 2 = 18
17.	× 2 = 10
18.	× 2 = 4
19.	× 2 = 6
20.	× 2 = 20

Score ____ / 20

Wednesday

Time allowed: minutes

1.	2 × = 20
2.	2 × = 12
3.	2 × = 4
4.	2 × = 10
5.	2 × = 18
6.	2 × = 2
7.	2 × = 14
8.	2 × = 8
9.	2 × = 6
10.	2 × = 16
11.	2 × = 10
12.	2 × = 18
13.	2 × = 4
14.	2 × = 8
15.	2 × = 2
16.	2 × = 12
17.	2 × = 6
18.	2 × = 16
19.	2 × = 14
20.	2 × = 0

Score ____ / 20

Thursday

Time allowed: minutes

1.	14 ÷ 2 =
2.	10 ÷ 2 =
3.	16 ÷ 2 =
4.	12 ÷ 2 =
5.	6 ÷ 2 =
6.	18 ÷ 2 =
7.	8 ÷ 2 =
8.	2 ÷ 2 =
9.	4 ÷ 2 =
10.	20 ÷ 2 =
11.	16 ÷ 2 =
12.	18 ÷ 2 =
13.	6 ÷ 2 =
14.	4 ÷ 2 =
15.	20 ÷ 2 =
16.	14 ÷ 2 =
17.	10 ÷ 2 =
18.	2 ÷ 2 =
19.	12 ÷ 2 =
20.	8 ÷ 2 =

Score ____ / 20

Week 22

Multiplication and Division ×3, ÷3

Weekly Assessment ☹ ☐ 😐 ☐ ☺ ☐

	Monday	Tuesday	Wednesday	Thursday
	Time allowed: minutes	Time allowed: minutes	Time allowed: minutes	Time allowed: minutes
1.	10 × 3 =	× 3 = 30	3 × = 30	21 ÷ 3 =
2.	5 × 3 =	× 3 = 18	3 × = 9	6 ÷ 3 =
3.	0 × 3 =	× 3 = 12	3 × = 27	18 ÷ 3 =
4.	9 × 3 =	× 3 = 21	3 × = 12	27 ÷ 3 =
5.	4 × 3 =	× 3 = 6	3 × = 3	9 ÷ 3 =
6.	6 × 3 =	× 3 = 15	3 × = 21	15 ÷ 3 =
7.	8 × 3 =	× 3 = 27	3 × = 15	24 ÷ 3 =
8.	2 × 3 =	× 3 = 3	3 × = 24	3 ÷ 3 =
9.	3 × 3 =	× 3 = 9	3 × = 6	12 ÷ 3 =
10.	7 × 3 =	× 3 = 24	3 × = 18	30 ÷ 3 =
11.	8 × 3 =	× 3 = 6	3 × = 0	18 ÷ 3 =
12.	1 × 3 =	× 3 = 27	3 × = 9	24 ÷ 3 =
13.	10 × 3 =	× 3 = 0	3 × = 21	27 ÷ 3 =
14.	5 × 3 =	× 3 = 18	3 × = 6	15 ÷ 3 =
15.	2 × 3 =	× 3 = 24	3 × = 30	30 ÷ 3 =
16.	7 × 3 =	× 3 = 9	3 × = 18	6 ÷ 3 =
17.	4 × 3 =	× 3 = 21	3 × = 24	12 ÷ 3 =
18.	9 × 3 =	× 3 = 15	3 × = 12	21 ÷ 3 =
19.	6 × 3 =	× 3 = 30	3 × = 27	3 ÷ 3 =
20.	3 × 3 =	× 3 = 12	3 × = 15	9 ÷ 3 =
	Score ___ / 20	Score ___ / 20	Score ___ / 20	Score ___ / 20

Week 23

Multiplication and Division ×4, ÷4

Weekly Assessment ☹ ☐ 😐 ☐ ☺ ☐

Monday	Tuesday	Wednesday	Thursday
Time allowed: minutes	Time allowed: minutes	Time allowed: minutes	Time allowed: minutes
1. 10 × 4 =	1. × 4 = 40	1. 4 × = 40	1. 16 ÷ 4 =
2. 3 × 4 =	2. × 4 = 20	2. 4 × = 16	2. 28 ÷ 4 =
3. 5 × 4 =	3. × 4 = 4	3. 4 × = 32	3. 4 ÷ 4 =
4. 0 × 4 =	4. × 4 = 36	4. 4 × = 8	4. 24 ÷ 4 =
5. 9 × 4 =	5. × 4 = 12	5. 4 × = 20	5. 36 ÷ 4 =
6. 7 × 4 =	6. × 4 = 24	6. 4 × = 4	6. 12 ÷ 4 =
7. 4 × 4 =	7. × 4 = 32	7. 4 × = 12	7. 20 ÷ 4 =
8. 8 × 4 =	8. × 4 = 8	8. 4 × = 28	8. 8 ÷ 4 =
9. 2 × 4 =	9. × 4 = 16	9. 4 × = 24	9. 40 ÷ 4 =
10. 6 × 4 =	10. × 4 = 28	10. 4 × = 36	10. 32 ÷ 4 =
11. 4 × 4 =	11. × 4 = 40	11. 4 × = 8	11. 36 ÷ 4 =
12. 7 × 4 =	12. × 4 = 0	12. 4 × = 28	12. 24 ÷ 4 =
13. 5 × 4 =	13. × 4 = 20	13. 4 × = 12	13. 40 ÷ 4 =
14. 10 × 4 =	14. × 4 = 8	14. 4 × = 16	14. 8 ÷ 4 =
15. 2 × 4 =	15. × 4 = 28	15. 4 × = 0	15. 32 ÷ 4 =
16. 6 × 4 =	16. × 4 = 4	16. 4 × = 24	16. 16 ÷ 4 =
17. 8 × 4 =	17. × 4 = 24	17. 4 × = 32	17. 4 ÷ 4 =
18. 1 × 4 =	18. × 4 = 16	18. 4 × = 40	18. 20 ÷ 4 =
19. 3 × 4 =	19. × 4 = 32	19. 4 × = 20	19. 12 ÷ 4 =
20. 9 × 4 =	20. × 4 = 12	20. 4 × = 4	20. 28 ÷ 4 =
Score ___ / 20	Score ___ / 20	Score ___ / 20	Score ___ / 20

Week 24

Multiplication and Division ×5, ÷5

Weekly Assessment ☹ ☐ 😐 ☐ ☺ ☐

Monday

Time allowed: minutes

1.	10 × 5 =
2.	5 × 5 =
3.	2 × 5 =
4.	9 × 5 =
5.	0 × 5 =
6.	6 × 5 =
7.	3 × 5 =
8.	7 × 5 =
9.	4 × 5 =
10.	8 × 5 =
11.	1 × 5 =
12.	6 × 5 =
13.	8 × 5 =
14.	2 × 5 =
15.	7 × 5 =
16.	5 × 5 =
17.	3 × 5 =
18.	10 × 5 =
19.	9 × 5 =
20.	4 × 5 =

Score ___ / 20

Tuesday

Time allowed: minutes

1.	× 5 = 50
2.	× 5 = 15
3.	× 5 = 30
4.	× 5 = 10
5.	× 5 = 25
6.	× 5 = 40
7.	× 5 = 0
8.	× 5 = 35
9.	× 5 = 20
10.	× 5 = 45
11.	× 5 = 10
12.	× 5 = 25
13.	× 5 = 5
14.	× 5 = 35
15.	× 5 = 45
16.	× 5 = 30
17.	× 5 = 20
18.	× 5 = 40
19.	× 5 = 50
20.	× 5 = 15

Score ___ / 20

Wednesday

Time allowed: minutes

1.	5 × = 50
2.	5 × = 30
3.	5 × = 0
4.	5 × = 40
5.	5 × = 15
6.	5 × = 20
7.	5 × = 45
8.	5 × = 10
9.	5 × = 25
10.	5 × = 35
11.	5 × = 20
12.	5 × = 45
13.	5 × = 15
14.	5 × = 40
15.	5 × = 30
16.	5 × = 10
17.	5 × = 50
18.	5 × = 25
19.	5 × = 35
20.	5 × = 5

Score ___ / 20

Thursday

Time allowed: minutes

1.	35 ÷ 5 =
2.	25 ÷ 5 =
3.	45 ÷ 5 =
4.	5 ÷ 5 =
5.	40 ÷ 5 =
6.	10 ÷ 5 =
7.	30 ÷ 5 =
8.	15 ÷ 5 =
9.	20 ÷ 5 =
10.	50 ÷ 5 =
11.	35 ÷ 5 =
12.	10 ÷ 5 =
13.	30 ÷ 5 =
14.	40 ÷ 5 =
15.	15 ÷ 5 =
16.	25 ÷ 5 =
17.	50 ÷ 5 =
18.	5 ÷ 5 =
19.	20 ÷ 5 =
20.	45 ÷ 5 =

Score ___ / 20

Week 25

Multiplication and Division ×6, ÷6

Weekly Assessment ☹ ☐ 😐 ☐ ☺ ☐

Monday

Time allowed: minutes

1.	10 × 6 =
2.	2 × 6 =
3.	8 × 6 =
4.	3 × 6 =
5.	9 × 6 =
6.	5 × 6 =
7.	4 × 6 =
8.	6 × 6 =
9.	0 × 6 =
10.	7 × 6 =
11.	1 × 6 =
12.	5 × 6 =
13.	8 × 6 =
14.	10 × 6 =
15.	6 × 6 =
16.	9 × 6 =
17.	3 × 6 =
18.	7 × 6 =
19.	2 × 6 =
20.	4 × 6 =

Score ___ / 20

Tuesday

Time allowed: minutes

1.	___ × 6 = 60
2.	___ × 6 = 36
3.	___ × 6 = 12
4.	___ × 6 = 6
5.	___ × 6 = 42
6.	___ × 6 = 18
7.	___ × 6 = 54
8.	___ × 6 = 24
9.	___ × 6 = 30
10.	___ × 6 = 48
11.	___ × 6 = 60
12.	___ × 6 = 0
13.	___ × 6 = 42
14.	___ × 6 = 30
15.	___ × 6 = 54
16.	___ × 6 = 6
17.	___ × 6 = 36
18.	___ × 6 = 12
19.	___ × 6 = 24
20.	___ × 6 = 48

Score ___ / 20

Wednesday

Time allowed: minutes

1.	6 × ___ = 60
2.	6 × ___ = 12
3.	6 × ___ = 0
4.	6 × ___ = 36
5.	6 × ___ = 6
6.	6 × ___ = 42
7.	6 × ___ = 18
8.	6 × ___ = 48
9.	6 × ___ = 24
10.	6 × ___ = 54
11.	6 × ___ = 30
12.	6 × ___ = 12
13.	6 × ___ = 24
14.	6 × ___ = 48
15.	6 × ___ = 0
16.	6 × ___ = 60
17.	6 × ___ = 6
18.	6 × ___ = 42
19.	6 × ___ = 18
20.	6 × ___ = 54

Score ___ / 20

Thursday

Time allowed: minutes

1.	36 ÷ 6 =
2.	6 ÷ 6 =
3.	42 ÷ 6 =
4.	12 ÷ 6 =
5.	54 ÷ 6 =
6.	24 ÷ 6 =
7.	48 ÷ 6 =
8.	30 ÷ 6 =
9.	18 ÷ 6 =
10.	60 ÷ 6 =
11.	36 ÷ 6 =
12.	42 ÷ 6 =
13.	6 ÷ 6 =
14.	60 ÷ 6 =
15.	12 ÷ 6 =
16.	48 ÷ 6 =
17.	30 ÷ 6 =
18.	18 ÷ 6 =
19.	54 ÷ 6 =
20.	24 ÷ 6 =

Score ___ / 20

Week 26

Multiplication and Division ×7, ÷7

Weekly Assessment ☹ ☐ 😐 ☐ ☺ ☐

Monday

Time allowed: 1:28 minutes

1.	1	×	7	=	7
2.	10	×	7	=	70
3.	5	×	7	=	35
4.	2	×	7	=	14
5.	7	×	7	=	49
6.	3	×	7	=	21
7.	8	×	7	=	56
8.	6	×	7	=	42
9.	4	×	7	=	28
10.	9	×	7	=	63
11.	5	×	7	=	35
12.	6	×	7	=	42
13.	2	×	7	=	14
14.	8	×	7	=	56
15.	3	×	7	=	21
16.	7	×	7	=	49
17.	9	×	7	=	63
18.	4	×	7	=	28
19.	10	×	7	=	70
20.	0	×	7	=	0

Score ___ / 20

Tuesday

148 15 28

Time allowed: minutes

1.	10	×	7	=	70
2.	2	×	7	=	14
3.	3	×	7	=	21
4.	5	×	7	=	35
5.	6	×	7	=	42
6.	1	×	7	=	7
7.	8	×	7	=	56
8.	4	×	7	=	28
9.	9	×	7	=	63
10.	7	×	7	=	49
11.	0	×	7	=	0
12.	5	×	7	=	35
13.	2	×	7	=	14
14.	4	×	7	=	28
15.	7	×	7	=	49
16.	1	×	7	=	7
17.	3	×	7	=	21
18.	8	×	7	=	56
19.	6	×	7	=	42
20.	9	×	7	=	63

Score ___ / 20

Wednesday

Time allowed: minutes

1.	7	×	10	=	70
2.	7	×	2	=	14
3.	7	×	0	=	0
4.	7	×	5	=	35
5.	7	×	3	=	21
6.	7	×	6	=	42
7.	7	×	4	=	28
8.	7	×	8	=	56
9.	7	×	7	=	49
10.	7	×	9	=	63
11.	7	×	1	=	7
12.	7	×	0	=	0
13.	7	×	4	=	28
14.	7	×	2	=	14
15.	7	×	10	=	70
16.	7	×	8	=	56
17.	7	×	3	=	21
18.	7	×	9	=	63
19.	7	×	5	=	35
20.	7	×	6	=	42

Score ___ / 20

Thursday

Time allowed: minutes

1.	14	÷	7	=	
2.	28	÷	7	=	
3.	7	÷	7	=	
4.	21	÷	7	=	
5.	56	÷	7	=	
6.	42	÷	7	=	
7.	63	÷	7	=	
8.	35	÷	7	=	
9.	49	÷	7	=	
10.	70	÷	7	=	
11.	42	÷	7	=	
12.	7	÷	7	=	
13.	56	÷	7	=	
14.	14	÷	7	=	
15.	63	÷	7	=	
16.	35	÷	7	=	
17.	21	÷	7	=	
18.	70	÷	7	=	
19.	49	÷	7	=	
20.	28	÷	7	=	

Score ___ / 20

Week 27

Multiplication and Division ×8, ÷8

Weekly Assessment ☹ ☐ 😐 ☐ ☺ ☐

Monday

Time allowed: minutes

1.	3 × 8 =
2.	10 × 8 =
3.	4 × 8 =
4.	2 × 8 =
5.	5 × 8 =
6.	8 × 8 =
7.	0 × 8 =
8.	9 × 8 =
9.	6 × 8 =
10.	7 × 8 =
11.	1 × 8 =
12.	4 × 8 =
13.	2 × 8 =
14.	5 × 8 =
15.	3 × 8 =
16.	6 × 8 =
17.	8 × 8 =
18.	7 × 8 =
19.	10 × 8 =
20.	9 × 8 =

Score ___ / 20

Tuesday

Time allowed: minutes

1.	× 8 = 80
2.	× 8 = 24
3.	× 8 = 0
4.	× 8 = 40
5.	× 8 = 16
6.	× 8 = 32
7.	× 8 = 56
8.	× 8 = 72
9.	× 8 = 48
10.	× 8 = 64
11.	× 8 = 8
12.	× 8 = 40
13.	× 8 = 48
14.	× 8 = 80
15.	× 8 = 16
16.	× 8 = 64
17.	× 8 = 0
18.	× 8 = 24
19.	× 8 = 32
20.	× 8 = 56

Score ___ / 20

Wednesday

Time allowed: minutes

1.	8 × = 80
2.	8 × = 16
3.	8 × = 24
4.	8 × = 40
5.	8 × = 8
6.	8 × = 48
7.	8 × = 32
8.	8 × = 64
9.	8 × = 56
10.	8 × = 72
11.	8 × = 0
12.	8 × = 80
13.	8 × = 40
14.	8 × = 32
15.	8 × = 8
16.	8 × = 48
17.	8 × = 72
18.	8 × = 56
19.	8 × = 24
20.	8 × = 64

Score ___ / 20

Thursday

Time allowed: minutes

1.	16 ÷ 8 =
2.	8 ÷ 8 =
3.	24 ÷ 8 =
4.	40 ÷ 8 =
5.	32 ÷ 8 =
6.	56 ÷ 8 =
7.	72 ÷ 8 =
8.	48 ÷ 8 =
9.	64 ÷ 8 =
10.	80 ÷ 8 =
11.	8 ÷ 8 =
12.	24 ÷ 8 =
13.	16 ÷ 8 =
14.	40 ÷ 8 =
15.	80 ÷ 8 =
16.	56 ÷ 8 =
17.	32 ÷ 8 =
18.	64 ÷ 8 =
19.	48 ÷ 8 =
20.	72 ÷ 8 =

Score ___ / 20

Week 28

Multiplication and Division ×9, ÷9

Weekly Assessment ☹ ☐ 😐 ☐ ☺ ☐

Monday

Time allowed: minutes

1.	1 × 9 = _
2.	5 × 9 = _
3.	2 × 9 = _
4.	4 × 9 = _
5.	3 × 9 = _
6.	7 × 9 = _
7.	6 × 9 = _
8.	9 × 9 = _
9.	10 × 9 = _
10.	8 × 9 = _
11.	3 × 9 = _
12.	1 × 9 = _
13.	4 × 9 = _
14.	2 × 9 = _
15.	0 × 9 = _
16.	5 × 9 = _
17.	9 × 9 = _
18.	7 × 9 = _
19.	8 × 9 = _
20.	6 × 9 = _

Score ___ / 20

Tuesday

Time allowed: minutes

1.	_ × 9 = 90
2.	_ × 9 = 18
3.	_ × 9 = 27
4.	_ × 9 = 36
5.	_ × 9 = 0
6.	_ × 9 = 54
7.	_ × 9 = 45
8.	_ × 9 = 72
9.	_ × 9 = 63
10.	_ × 9 = 81
11.	_ × 9 = 9
12.	_ × 9 = 18
13.	_ × 9 = 90
14.	_ × 9 = 27
15.	_ × 9 = 45
16.	_ × 9 = 63
17.	_ × 9 = 36
18.	_ × 9 = 72
19.	_ × 9 = 54
20.	_ × 9 = 81

Score ___ / 20

Wednesday

Time allowed: minutes

1.	9 × _ = 18
2.	9 × _ = 90
3.	9 × _ = 0
4.	9 × _ = 27
5.	9 × _ = 45
6.	9 × _ = 36
7.	9 × _ = 63
8.	9 × _ = 81
9.	9 × _ = 54
10.	9 × _ = 72
11.	9 × _ = 9
12.	9 × _ = 18
13.	9 × _ = 90
14.	9 × _ = 45
15.	9 × _ = 27
16.	9 × _ = 54
17.	9 × _ = 36
18.	9 × _ = 81
19.	9 × _ = 72
20.	9 × _ = 63

Score ___ / 20

Thursday

Time allowed: minutes

1.	9 ÷ 9 = _
2.	18 ÷ 9 = _
3.	36 ÷ 9 = _
4.	27 ÷ 9 = _
5.	45 ÷ 9 = _
6.	72 ÷ 9 = _
7.	54 ÷ 9 = _
8.	81 ÷ 9 = _
9.	63 ÷ 9 = _
10.	90 ÷ 9 = _
11.	18 ÷ 9 = _
12.	27 ÷ 9 = _
13.	9 ÷ 9 = _
14.	45 ÷ 9 = _
15.	90 ÷ 9 = _
16.	54 ÷ 9 = _
17.	81 ÷ 9 = _
18.	63 ÷ 9 = _
19.	36 ÷ 9 = _
20.	72 ÷ 9 = _

Score ___ / 20

Week 29

Multiplication and Division × 10, ÷ 10

Weekly Assessment ☹ ☐ 😐 ☐ ☺ ☐

Monday

Time allowed: minutes

1.	1 × 10 =
2.	9 × 10 =
3.	2 × 10 =
4.	4 × 10 =
5.	10 × 10 =
6.	3 × 10 =
7.	8 × 10 =
8.	5 × 10 =
9.	7 × 10 =
10.	6 × 10 =
11.	0 × 10 =
12.	4 × 10 =
13.	1 × 10 =
14.	7 × 10 =
15.	10 × 10 =
16.	6 × 10 =
17.	3 × 10 =
18.	9 × 10 =
19.	2 × 10 =
20.	8 × 10 =

Score ____ / 20

Tuesday

Time allowed: minutes

1.	× 10 = 100
2.	× 10 = 50
3.	× 10 = 30
4.	× 10 = 60
5.	× 10 = 90
6.	× 10 = 40
7.	× 10 = 70
8.	× 10 = 10
9.	× 10 = 20
10.	× 10 = 80
11.	× 10 = 20
12.	× 10 = 70
13.	× 10 = 30
14.	× 10 = 0
15.	× 10 = 60
16.	× 10 = 10
17.	× 10 = 80
18.	× 10 = 50
19.	× 10 = 90
20.	× 10 = 40

Score ____ / 20

Wednesday

Time allowed: minutes

1.	10 × = 10
2.	10 × = 100
3.	10 × = 60
4.	10 × = 50
5.	10 × = 80
6.	10 × = 20
7.	10 × = 90
8.	10 × = 40
9.	10 × = 70
10.	10 × = 30
11.	10 × = 10
12.	10 × = 60
13.	10 × = 50
14.	10 × = 90
15.	10 × = 20
16.	10 × = 40
17.	10 × = 0
18.	10 × = 80
19.	10 × = 30
20.	10 × = 70

Score ____ / 20

Thursday

Time allowed: minutes

1.	10 ÷ 10 =
2.	90 ÷ 10 =
3.	20 ÷ 10 =
4.	60 ÷ 10 =
5.	30 ÷ 10 =
6.	70 ÷ 10 =
7.	40 ÷ 10 =
8.	80 ÷ 10 =
9.	50 ÷ 10 =
10.	100 ÷ 10 =
11.	30 ÷ 10 =
12.	10 ÷ 10 =
13.	70 ÷ 10 =
14.	20 ÷ 10 =
15.	100 ÷ 10 =
16.	40 ÷ 10 =
17.	90 ÷ 10 =
18.	50 ÷ 10 =
19.	80 ÷ 10 =
20.	60 ÷ 10 =

Score ____ / 20

Week 30

Look Back

Weekly Assessment ☹ ☐ 😐 ☐ ☺ ☐

Monday

Time allowed: minutes

1.	5 × 2 =
2.	3 × 2 =
3.	6 × 4 =
4.	5 × 4 =
5.	5 × 8 =
6.	7 × 2 =
7.	9 × 2 =
8.	7 × 4 =
9.	4 × 8 =
10.	6 × 8 =
11.	6 × 2 =
12.	8 × 4 =
13.	8 × 2 =
14.	4 × 2 =
15.	4 × 4 =
16.	8 × 8 =
17.	3 × 4 =
18.	9 × 4 =
19.	7 × 8 =
20.	9 × 8 =

Score ___ / 20

Tuesday

Time allowed: minutes

1.	× 5 = 25
2.	× 5 = 50
3.	× 5 = 0
4.	× 10 = 80
5.	× 10 = 100
6.	× 10 = 20
7.	× 5 = 20
8.	× 5 = 45
9.	× 10 = 70
10.	× 10 = 50
11.	× 10 = 0
12.	× 10 = 90
13.	× 10 = 30
14.	× 5 = 15
15.	× 5 = 35
16.	× 5 = 5
17.	× 10 = 60
18.	× 10 = 40
19.	× 5 = 40
20.	× 5 = 30

Score ___ / 20

Wednesday

Time allowed: minutes

1.	3 × = 12
2.	3 × = 9
3.	6 × = 36
4.	6 × = 24
5.	3 × = 0
6.	3 × = 27
7.	6 × = 18
8.	6 × = 30
9.	9 × = 63
10.	3 × = 24
11.	6 × = 54
12.	9 × = 45
13.	3 × = 18
14.	6 × = 48
15.	9 × = 72
16.	9 × = 54
17.	3 × = 15
18.	3 × = 21
19.	9 × = 36
20.	9 × = 81

Score ___ / 20

Thursday

Time allowed: minutes

1.	× 7 = 14
2.	× 7 = 21
3.	× 7 = 0
4.	× 7 = 28
5.	× 7 = 7
6.	× 7 = 42
7.	7 × = 0
8.	7 × = 28
9.	7 × = 14
10.	7 × = 21
11.	7 × = 7
12.	7 × = 49
13.	× 7 = 35
14.	× 7 = 63
15.	× 7 = 49
16.	× 7 = 56
17.	7 × = 42
18.	7 × = 63
19.	7 × = 35
20.	7 × = 56

Score ___ / 20

Check-up 4

	A		B		C		D
1.	6 × 2 =	1.	4 × = 32	1.	× 2 = 18	1.	24 ÷ 4 =
2.	4 × 4 =	2.	3 × = 18	2.	× 3 = 24	2.	49 ÷ 7 =
3.	5 × 3 =	3.	5 × = 35	3.	× 5 = 45	3.	56 ÷ 8 =
4.	4 × 5 =	4.	2 × = 16	4.	× 4 = 36	4.	27 ÷ 9 =
5.	5 × 10 =	5.	8 × = 32	5.	× 10 = 100	5.	21 ÷ 3 =
6.	5 × 8 =	6.	6 × = 36	6.	× 6 = 54	6.	35 ÷ 5 =
7.	3 × 6 =	7.	8 × = 64	7.	× 8 = 72	7.	36 ÷ 4 =
8.	4 × 7 =	8.	7 × = 56	8.	× 7 = 21	8.	18 ÷ 2 =
9.	3 × 9 =	9.	9 × = 81	9.	× 9 = 63	9.	36 ÷ 6 =
10.	8 × 7 =	10.	5 × = 40	10.	× 8 = 32	10.	100 ÷ 10 =

Score ___ / 40

How did you do?